MATT
KENSETH

by Connie Colwell Miller

NASCAR
HEROES

Published by ABDO Publishing Company, PO Box 398166, Minneapolis, MN
55439. Copyright © 2013 by Abdo Consulting Group, Inc. International
copyrights reserved in all countries. No part of this book may be
reproduced in any form without written permission from the publisher.
SportsZone™ is a trademark and logo of ABDO Publishing Company.

Printed in the United States of America,
North Mankato, Minnesota
112012
012013

 THIS BOOK CONTAINS AT LEAST 10% RECYCLED MATERIALS.

Editor: Chrös McDougall
Series Designer: Becky Daum

Photo Credits: Autostock, Nigel Kinrade/AP Images, cover, title;
Autostock, Russell LaBounty/AP Images, cover, 27, 28-29; Bob Jordan/
AP Images, 4-5, 6-7, 30 (bottom); Chuck Burton/AP Images, 7, 15, 30
(center); The Capital Times, Michelle Stocker/AP Images, 8-9; ISC Images
& Archives/Getty Images, 10-11; David Taylor/Allsport/Getty Images,
12-13; Terry Renna/AP Images, 13; Robert Laberge/Allsport/Getty
Images, 14, 30 (top); Joe Cavaretta/AP Images, 16-17; Mary Altaffer/
AP Images, 18-19; Paul Kizzle/AP Images, 20-21; Will Lester/AP Images,
22-23, 31; John Raoux/AP Images, 24-25; Ralph Lauer/AP Images, 26

Cataloging-in-Publication Data
Colwell Miller, Connie.
 Matt Kenseth / Connie Colwell Miller.
   p. cm. -- (NASCAR heroes)
Includes bibliographical references and index.
ISBN 978-1-61783-665-7
1. Kenseth, Matt--Juvenile literature. 2. Automobile racing drivers--United
States--Biography--Juvenile literature. I. Title.
796.72092--dc21
[B]
                                                            2012946322

CONTENTS

Matt Kenseth (17) and Kasey Kahne (9) battle for position at the 2004 Subway 400 at North Carolina Speedway.

WINNING BY A HAIR

In 2004, National Association for Stock Car Auto Racing (NASCAR) driver Matt Kenseth zoomed around the North Carolina Speedway at the Subway 400. He was in the lead on the challenging track, but just barely. Kasey Kahne was in second place. And Kahne was trying hard to pass. But Kenseth would not budge.

FAST FACT

The North Carolina Speedway is nicknamed "the Rock" because of its challenging surface.

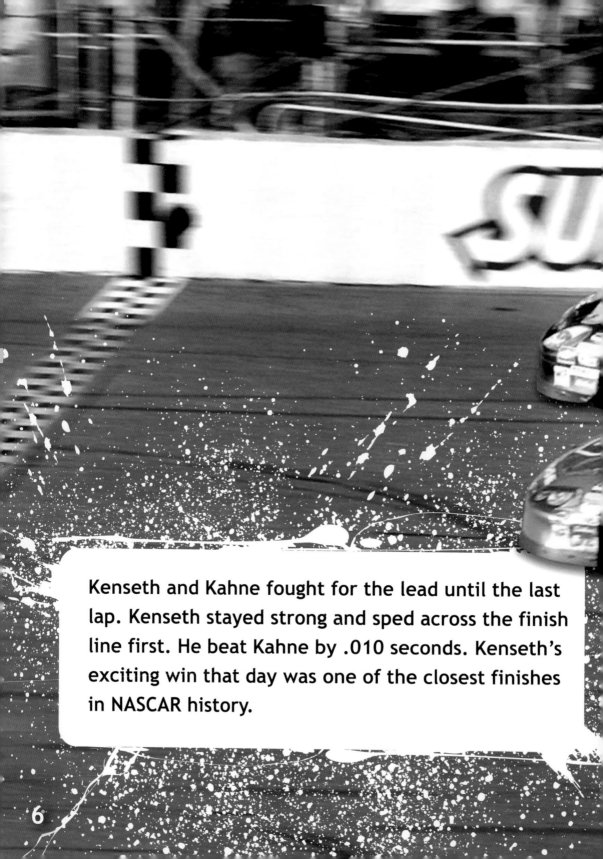

Kenseth and Kahne fought for the lead until the last lap. Kenseth stayed strong and sped across the finish line first. He beat Kahne by .010 seconds. Kenseth's exciting win that day was one of the closest finishes in NASCAR history.

Kenseth celebrates a narrow victory at the 2004 Subway 400.

Kenseth (yellow) edges Kahne at the finish line at the 2004 Subway 400.

Matt and his wife, Katie, ride atop a fire truck during a 2003 parade in his hometown.

FAST FACT

One of Matt Kenseth's nicknames is "Special K."

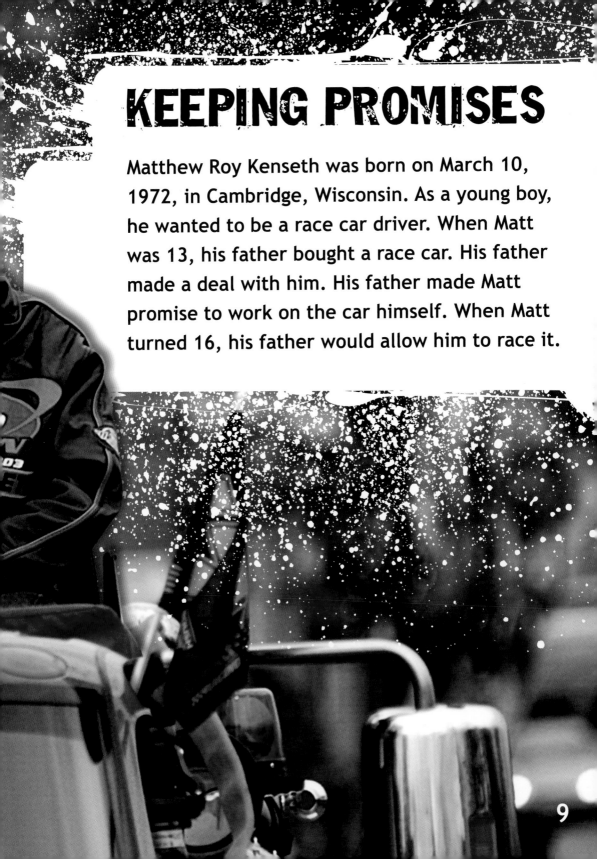

KEEPING PROMISES

Matthew Roy Kenseth was born on March 10, 1972, in Cambridge, Wisconsin. As a young boy, he wanted to be a race car driver. When Matt was 13, his father bought a race car. His father made a deal with him. His father made Matt promise to work on the car himself. When Matt turned 16, his father would allow him to race it.

When Matt turned 16, his father kept his promise. That year, Matt started racing. Before long, he started winning races. Matt won more and more challenging stock car races every year.

Kenseth (17) leads a pack during a 1998 NASCAR second-level series race at Daytona International Speedway.

FAST FACT

Matt Kenseth won the third feature race he entered. He was only a junior in high school.

MOVING UP

NASCAR team owner Robbie Reiser had his eye on Kenseth. In 1997, Reiser invited Kenseth to race in NASCAR's second-level series. Kenseth agreed. He raced only 21 races that year. He still came in second place for the Rookie of the Year Award.

FAST FACT

Before Robbie Reiser hired Matt Kenseth to race for his team, the two were fierce rivals in regional races in Wisconsin.

Robbie Reiser, left, and Kenseth in 2006

Kenseth races at Daytona
International Speedway in 1999.

Kenseth's performance proved he was ready for an even greater challenge. In 1998, he moved up to the NASCAR Cup Series. He raced just one race that year. But he finished in sixth place.

Kenseth raced a few more Cup Series races in 1999. By 2000, he was racing in the Cup Series full-time. He raced even better than the three years before. In fact, he won the Rookie of the Year Award for the Cup Series.

Kenseth races in the 2000 Brickyard 400.

Kenseth sprays Coke on his crew to celebrate winning the 2000 Coca-Cola 600.

FAST FACT

Matt Kenseth won his first Cup Series race in 2000. It was the Coca-Cola 600 in Concord, North Carolina.

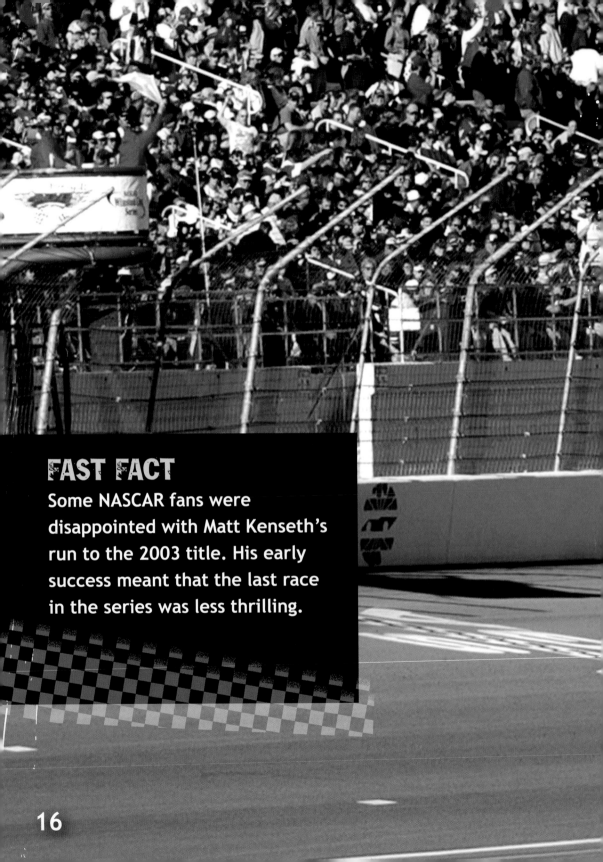

FAST FACT

Some NASCAR fans were disappointed with Matt Kenseth's run to the 2003 title. His early success meant that the last race in the series was less thrilling.

A DIFFERENT KIND OF CHAMP

Kenseth had his year in the spotlight in 2003. He won the Cup Series championship, and he did so with an amazing 25 top-10 finishes.

Kenseth gathered points for each of his strong finishes. His enormous number of points caused a problem for others. Soon no driver could possibly beat him. Kenseth won the championship before the Cup Series was even over.

Kenseth crosses the finish line first at a 2003 race at Las Vegas Motor Speedway.

The next year, NASCAR changed the way scores were figured. No longer could a driver win the championship before the final race. Kenseth's consistent finishes helped change the sport forever.

FAST FACT

Matt Kenseth won the 2003 Cup Series championship despite winning only a single race. He finished in the top 10 so many times that his point total was higher than any other driver's.

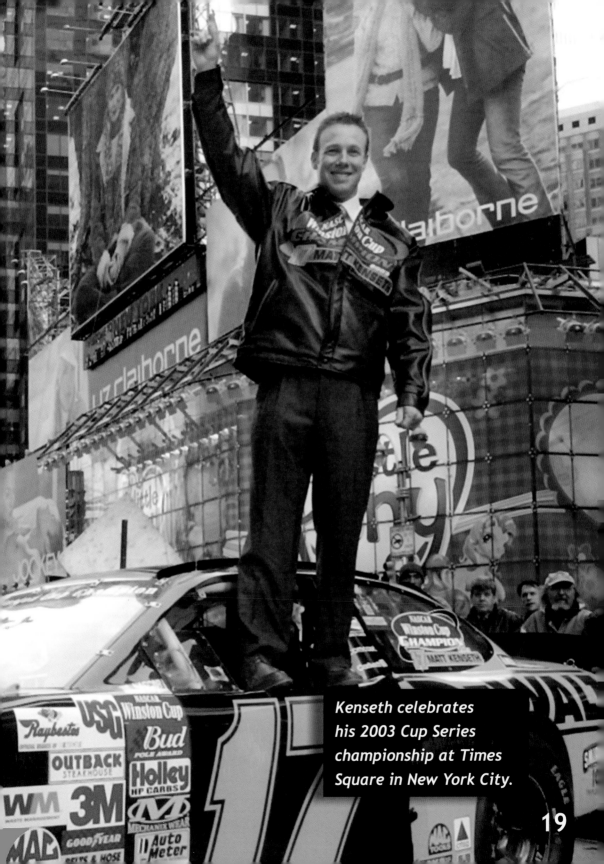

Kenseth celebrates his 2003 Cup Series championship at Times Square in New York City.

GOING STRONG

From 2004 to 2008, Kenseth kept his sights on the championship. He finished in the top 12 each year. It seemed that every winning driver had Kenseth hot on his tail.

Kenseth cruises at a 2008 race in Homestead, Florida.

FAST FACT

In 2007, Matt Kenseth tied Jimmie Johnson for the most top-10 Cup Series finishes in a row. Kenseth finished in the top 10 for six years straight, from 2002 to 2007.

Kenseth leads a 2009 race in Fontana, California.

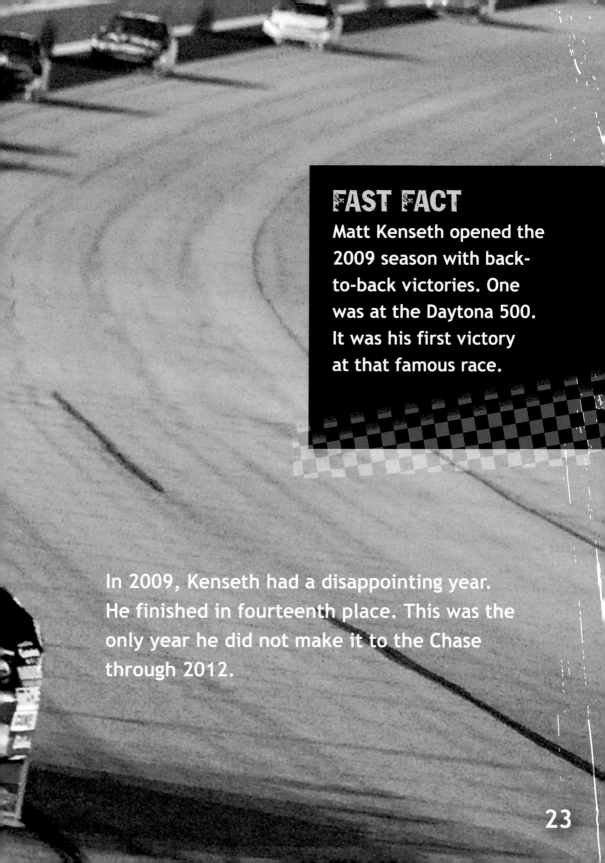

FAST FACT

Matt Kenseth opened the 2009 season with back-to-back victories. One was at the Daytona 500. It was his first victory at that famous race.

In 2009, Kenseth had a disappointing year. He finished in fourteenth place. This was the only year he did not make it to the Chase through 2012.

FAST FACT

Matt Kenseth has a pilot's
license. He sometimes
flies himself to races.

*Kenseth (17) leads a pack
during a practice session for
the 2010 Daytona 500.*

In 2010, Kenseth was back in action. He finished fifth in the Cup Series. In 2011, he finished fourth. It seemed Kenseth was again at the top of the NASCAR field.

MR. CONSISTENCY

Kenseth's fans often call him "Mr. Consistency." This nickname refers to his tendency to almost always be in the running for wins. It seems that if Kenseth is not winning, he is usually close behind.

In his first 12 full years of racing, Kenseth won 21 Cup Series races. He had an incredible 113 top-five finishes. In eight of his first 12 full years, Kenseth finished in the top 10 in the race for the championship.

In 2007, Matt Kenseth did not win the Cup Series championship. But he led more laps (624) than any other driver in the Chase for the Cup that season.

Kenseth leads Carl Edwards at a 2012 Cup Series race in Dover, Delaware.

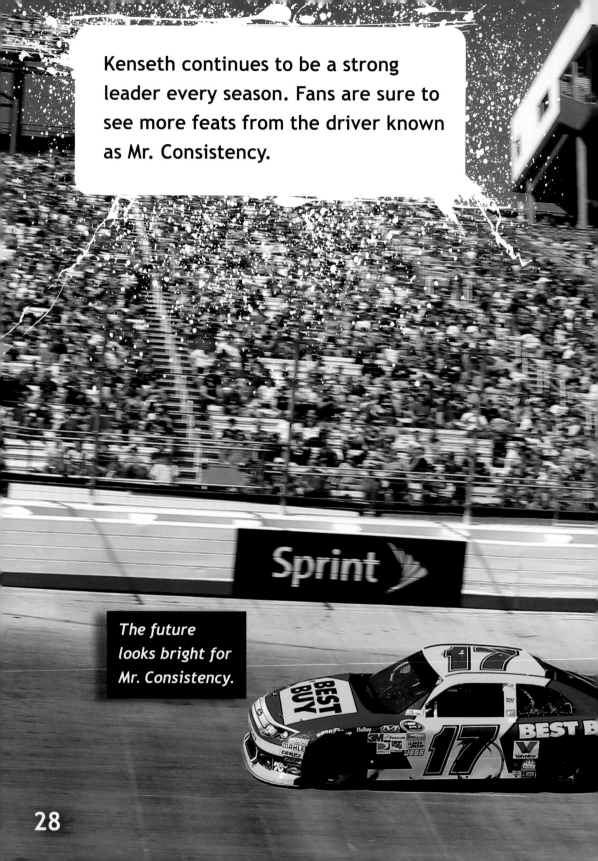

Kenseth continues to be a strong leader every season. Fans are sure to see more feats from the driver known as Mr. Consistency.

The future looks bright for Mr. Consistency.

FAST FACT

Matt Kenseth won the Daytona 500 for the second time in 2012.

TIMELINE

1972
Matthew Roy Kenseth is born on March 10 in Cambridge, Wisconsin.

1997
Kenseth drives in 21 races on NASCAR's second-level series.

1998
Kenseth competes in his first NASCAR Cup Series race.

2000
Kenseth marries Katie Martin.

2000
Kenseth wins the Cup Series Rookie of the Year Award.

2003
Kenseth wins the Cup Series championship.

2009
Kenseth wins the Daytona 500.

2012
Kenseth wins the Daytona 500 for the second time.

GLOSSARY

Chase
The last 10 races of the NASCAR Cup Series. Only the top 10 drivers and two wild cards qualify to race in the Chase.

Cup Series
NASCAR's top series for professional stock car drivers. It has been called the Sprint Cup Series since 2008.

Daytona 500
The most famous stock car race in the world and one of the races in the Cup Series.

feature race
A stock car race on a short track. The drivers are not professionals.

rookie
A driver in his or her first full-time season in a new series.

second-level series
NASCAR's second-level series for professional stock car drivers. It has been called the Nationwide Series since 2008.

series
A racing season that consists of several races.

stock car
Race cars that resemble models of cars that people drive every day.

INDEX